Perfect World

How I Survived My Most EMBARRASSING Moments

TERRIFYING but **true** stories
of embarrassing moments
from kids just like you!

by ROBIN WASSERMAN

Illustrated by ANGELA MARTINI

Scholastic Inc.

New York   Toronto   London   Auckland   Sydney
Mexico City   New Delhi   Hong Kong   Buenos Aires

For **Alexis**,
a **true** and **lifelong** friend,
whether she's across the city
or across the country.

ISBN 0-439-68691-1

Copyright © 2004 by Scholastic Inc.
All rights reserved. Published by Scholastic Inc.
SCHOLASTIC and associated logos are trademarks and/or
registered trademarks of Scholastic Inc.

12 11 10 9 8 7 6 5 4 3 2 1   4 5 6 7 8 9/0

Printed in the U.S.A.
First printing, September 2004

Book design by Jennifer Rinaldi Windau

You think *you've* got problems?

Take it from me, being totally humiliated in front of 20 or 30 of your nearest and dearest just stinks.

There's no other word for it.

Okay, that's a lie. There are plenty of other words for it—being embarrassed is:

Terrible.

Atrocious.

Ghastly.

Abominable.

Horribly, horrendously, humiliatingly heinous.

And I should know.

Why? Because I've been there, more times than I can count. More times than I *want* to count. I've never met a staircase that didn't send me flying down headfirst, never played a game of volleyball that didn't end with me getting whacked in the head in front of my whole team, and *definitely* never talked to a cute boy without saying something that made me feel like an incredible, red-faced fool. But every dark cloud has a silver lining, and here's mine: I may know more about getting utterly humiliated than anyone in the world, so who better to give you advice?

Lesson #1: Misery loves company. Which is why I like to remind myself that I'm not the only one who completely embarrasses herself on a regular basis. And you know what? Neither are you. (Even if it may sometimes seem that way!)

That's why I've collected all these stories of other kids' embarrassing moments. Maybe reading about what they've gone through will make you feel better about your own horrifically humiliating moment. Or maybe it will just make you laugh and forget about your own problems for a few minutes. (After you've finished the book, you're allowed to crawl back under the covers and hide from the world again.) If nothing else, it will convince you that you're not alone. Embarrassment is a part of life—a stinky, painful, unfair, unpleasant, and pretty much atrocious part of life, but what can you do? Just keep reading, keep laughing . . . and maybe next time, watch where you're going!

HOW TO FIND YOUR
HUMILIATION QUOTIENT

Before we get started, let's talk ratings. You know—just how horrible *is* your horrible humiliation? After all, can tripping down the stairs *really* compare to wetting your pants in public? Um, no. So we're going to need a system that distinguishes between *"bad,"* *"really bad,"* and *"so bad I need to move to a different country."* Lucky for you, I've already come up with one—complete with a handy guide for how you can rate your own real-life embarrassing moments, along with the ones in this book. Check it out:

*Circle the answers that apply
to your unfortunate situation:*

1. When it happened, my face turned the color of

    a. cotton candy.

    b. a tomato.

    c. a beet.

2. I don't plan on leaving my room again until

    a. next week.

    b. next month.

    c. college.

3. I embarrassed myself in front of

    a. 5–10 people.

    b. 10–50 people.

    c. 50 or more people.

4. The laughter lasted

    a. 5 minutes.

    b. 10 minutes.

    c. forever!

5. My humiliation would best be called

    a. an embarrassing moment.

    b. a humiliating day.

    c. a daily walk of shame for several weeks until
       it (whatever it is) grew back/washed off/etc.

6. When I tell the story now

    a. I laugh.

    b. I still shiver in horror.

    c. Nothing could ever make me tell this story
       to anyone. Ever.

Now give yourself

1 point for every A,

2 points for every B, and

3 points for every C.

My HQ:
⟨humiliation quotient⟩

6-8: *Ridiculously Red-faced*

Come on, admit it, whatever
happened wasn't really that bad.
So stop whining and consider
yourself lucky—things could have
been much, much worse.
(Don't believe me? See below!)

9-11: *Moderate Mortification*

You may not die of shame,
but you'll certainly be
living in humiliation
for longer than you'd like.
Don't worry—people will forget.
Eventually.

12-14: X-Treme Embarrassment

You're so humiliated that you're
probably *still* blushing, right?
You can't hide under the covers
forever—but I can see why you'd want
to stay there for a few more days.
Or weeks.

15-18: Humiliation Horror

Oh. My. Gosh. I can't believe that happened to
you. What a nightmare—and I can see why
you're ready to hop on a plane, change your
identity, and leave this life behind forever. Or
at least stay in your room until college.
And who could blame you?

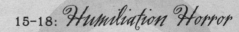

FALL FOOL

I DON'T KNOW ABOUT YOU, BUT I HATE THE FALL. The end of summer. The end of warm weather. The beginning of school. And you know what that means—lots more opportunities for total embarrassment, at least if you're anything like me. Think about it: Missing the ball in gym, spitting up food in the cafeteria, falling on your face in the playground . . . For these unlucky kids, the possibilities are endless!

Thar She Blows!

I've always been into science, so I was super-excited when my teacher decided we should do a real chemistry lab. Then she picked *me* to help her. There I was at the front of the classroom, in my lab coat and goggles, pouring all these chemicals from one beaker into another. Everything was going great, until I poured in the last ingredient . . . and the whole thing blew up in my face! My teacher and I were both covered in green goo. The class couldn't stop laughing. Fortunately, the chemicals weren't dangerous. The only thing hurt was my pride.

—Dana

HE SAYS . . . *Dude, science experiments gone wrong are always cool, and green goo is a definite plus. Rock on!*

3 Smells Like Teen Spirit

I wanted to look and smell extra special for the school's Fall Ball, so I decided to try some of my mother's perfume. I dabbed a little on my wrists, a little on my neck, and then I accidentally spilled the rest of the bottle all over myself. It smelled like I took a bath in the perfume! I did everything I could think of to get the smell off. I even took another shower. I thought I'd washed most of it off, but it turned out I still stank when I got to the dance. I smelled extra special, all right. So special that for the rest of the night, no one would come within ten feet of me.

—Claudia

Party Time . . . Not

YOU RATE IT! _____

Every time Meghan has a party, it rocks. So when she sent out the invitations for her birthday party this year, I was psyched to get invited. I couldn't wait. I was counting the days. But when I showed up at her door on Saturday night, none of the other kids were there. *Meghan* wasn't even there! It turns out I miscounted. But my parents had already dropped me off, and there was no one to pick me up until the end of the night. Would you believe I spent that Saturday night watching TV with Meghan's parents? The worst part was, when the party actually did happen, I was too embarrassed to go!

—**Lissa**

HIS Humiliation
Fool in School

I was starting middle school, and I was determined that this year was going to be a fresh start. New school, new cool reputation. My older sister had some first-day advice for me: Steer clear of the older guys. She said they liked to play practical jokes on the new kids. But I didn't listen. I fig-

ured I could take care of myself. I was wrong. As I was trying to get my locker open, a bunch of older guys snuck up behind me and shoved me inside, then they slammed the door shut and ran away! I shouted and yelled for help, but no one could get me out. The locker was locked, and I couldn't remember the combination! Eventually, someone had to get the janitor, and he finally let me out. I got my new reputation all right: total loser.

— Peter

Drat That Cat

When my friend got permission to bring her cat to school for science class, we were all so excited. After all, how often do you get to play with a cat in school? (My parents are allergic to fur, so the only pet I've ever been allowed to have is a fish.) We all got a chance to pet the cat, and I even got to hold it in my lap for a minute. It was great—until the cat threw up. All over me. It was the grossest thing I've ever seen. The teacher helped me wash it off, but it didn't *really* come off. I had to walk around in wet jeans smelling like cat puke until my mother could come pick me up, many, many hours later.

—**Jillian**

Hunger Pains

YOU RATE IT! _____

I had forgotten my lunch and didn't have any money with me to buy food, so I figured I would just wait until I got home to eat something. By the last class of the day, I was STARVING. I could barely wait for the class to be over and neither could my stomach. It started grumbling and rumbling in the middle of class. It didn't seem like anyone heard it, but I don't know how they could have missed it. To me, it sounded even louder than the teacher! Apparently, I wasn't the only one to think so. When the bell rang, the cute boy who sits next to me pulled a candy bar out of his backpack and handed it to me. "Sounds like you need this more than I do," he said, laughing. I couldn't look him in the eye for the rest of the semester!

—**Claire**

HE SAYS . . . FYI: Guys love girls who love to eat. And it sounds like this guy's got a little crush on you. Why not buy him a candy bar to pay him back?

Stick in the Mud

Sometimes on my way home from school, I take a shortcut through a field near my house. Usually it's empty. *Usually.* One day after soccer practice, I was cutting through  the field when suddenly, I heard something chasing after me. I thought I must be imagining it, but when I turned around there was a cow! I started running as fast as I could. Just before I got to the edge of the field, I slipped and fell—*splat* into a giant pile of mud and manure. I got up and got myself out of that field, *fast*. I was safe. I was also covered in mud. And I stank. I slunk home the rest of the way, just glad no one had been there to see me. But I should have known my luck wasn't that

15

good. When I got back to my house, a bunch of my friends were waiting there to see if I wanted to hang out. When they saw me, they burst into laughter and held their noses. Next time, it's the long way home for me.

—**Shannon**

Good Night, Sleep Tight

YOU RATE IT! _____

Last year in our school play I was a king, and in my first scene, I was supposed to be asleep in a forest. There was just one small problem: I fell asleep. Onstage. In front of all those people. A boy dressed in a tree costume had to inch up to the front of the stage and nudge me awake. By the time I opened my eyes, the audience was roaring with laughter. It was the beginning—and the ending—of my acting career.

—**Glory**

I Can Read (Trust Me!)

YOU RATE IT! _____

Every Friday afternoon at school, we have Sustained Silent Reading. We each have to bring in a book and then spend 40 minutes reading it. It's usually a pretty fun way to end the school week, except for the day that I accidentally brought my little brother's book to school instead of mine. So while everyone else was reading their chapter books, I had to sit there and read *The Happy Fire Engine*. The other kids in my class couldn't stop laughing at me. I was so embarrassed, and very bored. The book is so short that by the end of the day, I'd read it about 12 times in a row.

—Summer

HE SAYS . . .
The Happy Fire Engine?
Dude, I love that book!

Stink Alert!

We have one rule in our cooking class: You make it, you eat it. Unfortunately, I'm a very picky eater, so that just doesn't work for me. One day

we made fruit salad, and there was *no way* I was eating that. So when we were finished, I emptied my portion into the pocket of my apron, and then after class stuffed the apron into my locker. I totally forgot about it until the next day, when I got to school and discovered a bunch of people standing around my locker holding their noses. It turns out that when you leave fruit salad in a locker overnight, it starts to smell pretty funky. I threw out the fruit salad right away, but my locker stank for days!

—Susan

Snack Time

We keep our cat food in the refrigerator, right next to all of our human food. And the container looks just like a tuna fish container. One day, when I really wasn't paying attention, I  accidentally grabbed the cat food instead of the tuna fish. As soon as I took a bite, I realized exactly what I had done. But it was too late. I brushed my teeth about a million times and then called my best friend to tell her how horrified I was. Some friend she turned out to be. She thought it was so funny, she told the whole school that I eat cat food. By the end of the next day, everyone was calling me "Whiskers," and they still do!

—**Cheryl**

MEGA-BLUNDER!
Is There a Doctor in the House?

Every Tuesday and Thursday, I get a special treat for lunch: Vince, the boy I have a mega-crush on, eats at my table. Or at least, he did. Until that horrible, humiliating Tuesday when I choked on my mystery meat. For a minute, I really couldn't breathe. I didn't know what I was going to do! My friend pounded me on the back as hard as she could, and finally, I coughed up the mystery meat and spat it right out. I was so relieved until I looked across the table at Vince. There was my chewed-up mystery meat, splattered all over his face.

—Samantha

Making the Grade

When my teacher handed our tests back and I saw that I got a 70, I couldn't believe it! How could I have gotten a C– after studying so hard? My parents were going to kill me. I couldn't help it. I started to cry. I hoped no one would notice, but my teacher did, and she came over to see what was wrong. When I told her, she started laughing. It turns out that I didn't get a 70, I got a 90. I had just misread her handwriting. By that point, I was too embarrassed to be happy. But it was still a huge relief.

—Erica

Humiliation Helper

I don't know about you, but I tend to cry. **A LOT.**
And there's nothing more embarrassing than
crying in public. **I'm still looking for the perfect
solution**, but here's what I've got so far:

1. BITE your lip or the inside of your cheek.
2. HOLD your breath.
3. COUNT to 100 in your head—if possible, in a
   foreign language.
4. CLOSE your eyes and pretend you're at
   the beach.
5. Try to PICTURE the people around you
   dressed as clowns.
6. TAKE deep breaths.
7. COME UP with five things in your life you
   should be happy about.
8. BRIBE yourself with the promise of a treat if
   you can hold it together.
9. Try to RELAX all your tensed muscles.
10. FORCE yourself to smile—scientists claim
    that *looking* happy can actually make you
    feel happy!

Bon Appétit!

When my class baked brownies as a class project, it seemed like a great idea. Definitely better than a history project or a math test, right? But after my group had washed all our dishes, I noticed something: The Band-Aid that had been on my finger wasn't there anymore. Had it fallen off on the floor? In the sink? Or . . . in the brownies? Soon I got my answer. We pulled the brownies out of the oven and everyone got one to try. Everything was perfect, until I heard it: "Yuck!" Someone pulled a chocolate-covered, melty Band-Aid out of the middle of his brownie. Our teacher freaked out, and we had to throw all the brownies away. To this day, no one but me knows where the Band-Aid came from. But I live in fear that someday, somehow, someone will figure it out!

—Hannah

WINTER WORRIES

YOU CAN BUNDLE UP UNDER AS MANY LAYERS as you want to protect you from the cold, but they haven't invented a coat thick enough to protect you from the chill of humiliation. And 'tis the season for some wild winter disasters. Got a New Year's resolution yet? How about: NO MORE EMBARRASSING MOMENTS!

She Loves Me, She Loves Me Not

Every Valentine's Day at my school, we exchange valentines in homeroom. Everyone gets a few cards, but the really popular girls always get flowers or chocolates from all the boys with crushes on them. I've always dreamed of getting flowers for Valentine's Day. So you can imagine how excited I was this year, when a bouquet was delivered to my classroom—and it was for me! Then I opened the card, and guess what? They were from my *mother*. That would have been bad enough, but then the boy sitting next to me noticed the card: "To my dear Dizzy Lizzy, you will always be my valentine. Love and kisses, Mommy." Before I could stop him, he read it to the whole class. I guess it's true what they say— love hurts!

—Liz

Do-Si-Don't

My parents are big believers in family bonding. That means that every Saturday afternoon we have to spend some "quality time" together. Each week, a different person gets to pick the activity, and one

week my mother picked square-dancing lessons. Yes, that's right: *square-dancing lessons*. I couldn't believe it either. But you haven't heard the worst part yet. The dance studio was in the mall, next to my favorite store, and it had a giant glass window in front. I spent the first half of the lesson in misery, dreading the thought of anyone from school seeing me. But then I kind of got into it and started having fun. At the end of the lesson, we did this really complicated dance, and when we finished, I was feeling pretty proud of myself. And then I heard the applause. I turned around to look out the window—and there were a bunch of kids from my school staring at us, pointing, clapping, and, of course, laughing. I may never live it down!

—Maren

Hair Today, Gone Tomorrow

For a long time, my twin brother and I were in a practical joke war. Okay, I have to admit that I may have started it, but he definitely finished it. One day, after I had gone to bed, he snuck into my room, and he cut off clumps of my hair! He got grounded for a month, but his punishment wasn't nearly as bad as what I had to suffer through—walking around school half bald until my hair grew back in. I didn't speak to him until it did, months and months later.

—Trista

Spit It Out

I was at my second cousin's wedding, and I was bored out of my mind. I tried counting the lights on the ceiling, I tried making a mental list of all the people I knew, I even tried paying attention, but I was still falling asleep in total boredom. Eventually, I got so bored I just started blowing up my cheeks and swishing saliva from one to the other. (Hey, it gave me some-  thing to do!) Unfortunately, it turned out my little sister was just as bored as I was. When she saw my cheeks blown up, she smacked them, and before I could stop myself, my saliva flew out of my mouth and splattered onto the head of the guy sitting in front of us. I was totally humiliated, but I'm pretty sure my parents felt even worse!

—Lavinia

HE SAYS . . .
She spits, she scores!

Land of Make-Believe

I was hanging out with my little sister after school one day and we decided to play dress up.

I know I'm a little old for that sort of thing, but my sister loves it and I have to admit I was having some fun, too. She dressed up like a princess. Then she put a black pointy hat on my head and painted a big wart on my face so that I could be the wicked witch. I chased her out of the bedroom, through the hallway, and down the stairs—where I came face-to-face with the entire math club from school. They were coming over to practice for our Mega-Math Challenge, and I totally forgot. But trust me, I'll never forget anything again!

—Shavonne

Shake It Up

I had grabbed a soda out of the vending machine and was heading back to my cafeteria table when I totally tripped over my own two feet and fell. This wasn't the embarrassing part. I'm a huge klutz, and that sort of thing happens to me all the time. I've learned to ignore it. The soda

had rolled away, so I picked it up and finally made it back to my table. Then I opened the soda. Maybe I shouldn't have ignored my little fall after all. I must have shaken up the soda because when I opened it, it exploded all over me. I was wet, sticky, and humiliated for the rest of the day.

—Mindy

Get Me out of Here!

My dentist's office is in a giant office building that has big automatic revolving doors in the lobby. The last time I was there, my appointment was so horrible and painful that all I wanted to do was escape and get home as soon as possible. No such luck. As I was passing through the revolving doors, they froze. I pushed as hard as I could, but they wouldn't move. I was trapped! As the lobby filled up with people staring at me, I had to wait there for the building maintenance man to come and let me out. And I thought the *dentist* was painful!

—Kelly

Avalanche!

There are a few hundred kids in my school and in between classes, we all use the same flight of stairs. So it gets just a *little* crowded. And there's a *lot* of pushing. One day, I was trying to get down the stairs and someone behind me started pushing. Hard. I lost my balance and started toppling down the stairs. Fortunately, there were so many people in front of me that I didn't have far to fall. *Unfortunately*, when I fell on them, I knocked them off balance, and they started to topple, too! It was like a chain of dominoes. More and more and more people fell on top of each other until there was a giant pile of us down at the bottom. Lucky for me, no one got hurt. And even luckier for me, no one ever found out who caused the avalanche.

—Farah

Humiliation Helper

TOP 10 WAYS TO STOP BEING SUCH A KLUTZ

Sure, no one's *graceful* all the time, but let's face it:
In this world, there are those of us who walk
with our heads held high and then there are
those of us who **trip over our own two feet**.
Here's my 10-step plan to spend more time
on my feet and less time flat on my face:

1. **Pay more attention to where I'm going**.
2. **Keep my shoelaces tied** at all times.
3. Take **ballet lessons**.
4. Learn to **juggle**.
5. **Stop scuffing my feet** on the ground
   when I walk.
6. Try **yoga**.
7. **Practice walking** on a balance beam.
8. **Stop flinging my hands around** so much
   when I talk.
9. **Stop talking on my cell phone so much**
   while I walk.
10. **Pay more attention to where I'm going**.
    (*Yes, I know I already said that, but trust me, this
    is the one I'm most likely to forget.*)

Sing It Loud, Sing It Proud

YOU RATE IT! _____

I was taking a shower and singing my favorite
Britney Spears song at the top of my lungs. I may
never be a better singer than her, but I can definitely be louder than her. I was still singing when
I turned off the water, wrapped myself in a towel,
and opened the bathroom door. And there were
my sister and all of her friends, staring at me and
laughing. They still call me Britney, and somehow, I don't think it's a compliment.

—Bethany

Roach Motel

I was in the locker room after swim practice,

about to change back into my
clothes. But when I opened my
locker, I got a little surprise. A
giant cockroach crawled out of
my shoe! I shrieked and
slammed the door shut. Then I
ran away from the locker, away
from the locker room, and didn't stop until
I was safely out in the hallway. It was only then
that I realized I was standing in the middle of the
hallway of my school, surrounded by students,

wearing only a bathing suit. The humiliation was bad, but sticking my foot into a cockroach-stuffed shoe would have been much, much worse.

—Jamie

HE SAYS... Why are girls always so afraid of bugs? Bugs are awesome.

Dessert First

After we won our championship soccer game, I went out with my team to celebrate. Dinner was okay, but dessert was fabulous.

The restaurant had a sundae bar, and we each got to make our own. I filled my bowl up to the brim and stuck on every topping they had. Then I walked back to the table, careful not to spill it. I was focusing so much on the bowl of ice cream that I didn't notice the small step between me and the table. Not only did I trip and fall on my face, but I fell right in the ice cream. Everyone laughed, especially when I picked myself up and my face was covered by chocolate ice cream and sprinkles. That was enough sundae for me!

—Amaya

You're on the Air

Every morning, I listen to the "Mike and Tom" radio show. Everyone does. The DJs are great, and they always give away awesome prizes. One day, they were giving away free No Doubt tickets, and all you had to do to win them was call up and answer the easiest trivia question in the world: What is the name of No Doubt's lead singer? That's my favorite band, so I called and called, and finally, I got through! They put me on the air, and I was so excited. But I was also incredibly nervous. So nervous that when they asked me the trivia question, I totally blanked. I couldn't speak, or even think, and I definitely couldn't come up with the name of the lead singer. Eventually, they had to hang up on me and go to another caller. He knew the answer, of course: Gwen Stefani. *Everyone* knows that! Why couldn't I just say it? It was so embarrassing. Everyone from my school was listening and knew it was me! And they all knew this was one name that I should never have forgotten!

—**Gwen**

SPRING SLIPUPS

LOOKS LIKE SPRING HAS SPRUNG: BIRDS ARE singing, flowers are blooming, and everywhere you look, love is in the air. Unless you're looking in my direction, of course. Love may be in the air, but I'm such a klutz, it's most likely to hit me in the face! Guess I'm not the only one.

Hello and Good-bye

I was walking down the hall when Rick S., the cutest guy in school, waved at me. I couldn't believe that he knew who I was, and I guess I should have known it was too good to be true. It turns out that he was waving at the girl behind me. How do I know? Because she walked past me and threw her arms around him. Then she whispered something in his ear, pointed at me, and they both started laughing. I think my face turned redder than a tomato.

—Maria

HE SAYS . . . He's a jerk. She's a jerk. Sounds like you're better off without —and better than—both of them.

35

Humiliation Helper

TOP 10 WAYS TO PRETEND YOU
DON'T HAVE A CRUSH

So your *top secret crush* has accidentally spotted your top secret, never-supposed-to-be-sent love letters, and now he knows that your heart beats faster every time he's around? **Don't panic!** Before you die of embarrassment, here's how to fool the love of your life into thinking you have no interest whatsoever. NOTE: If you like a guy and you want him to like you, *this is NOT THE WAY TO GO.*

1. *Flirt* with other boys while he's watching.
2. Pretend you *forgot* his name.
3. Act *bored* when he talks to you.
4. Tell him you want to *set him up* with one of your friends.
5. *Ask* if he can set you up with one of *his* friends.
6. *Insult* his favorite sports team.
7. "*Forget*" to return his phone calls.
8. Talk to him about other guys you think are *cute*.
9. *Don't laugh* at his jokes—even if they're funny.
10. Offer him a breath mint and tell him *he needs it.*

And the Winner Is . . .

I was so excited to be nominated for homecoming queen in my middle school. But I'm pretty popular, so I guess I wasn't too surprised. All my friends were convinced that I would win and by the night of the homecoming dance, I was convinced, too. I crossed all my fingers and toes as they were about to announce the winner. It must have worked. They announced my name!

I raced up onto the stage . . . and it was only then that I realized they had only announced my *first* name. There was another girl nominated who was also named Julia, and she was the real winner. Or at least she's the one who got the crown and the flowers, while I slunk off the stage feeling like a giant lamebrain in front of my whole school.

—Julia

Say Cheese

It was picture day at school, so I wore my newest outfit and made sure that my hair looked absolutely perfect. Too bad it began to rain as I walked to school. It was bad enough that my clothes got wet and my hair got totally ruined. But then, a couple of blocks away from school, a truck drove by and spattered me with a tidal wave of muddy water. By the time I got to school, I looked like a drowned rat. This is one school picture that won't end up hanging on our refrigerator. I guarantee it.

—Bonnie

HIS Humiliation
The Great Outdoors

I'm not a big nature guy, so when I went on an overnight camping trip with my Scout troop, I was a little nervous. But at first everything went okay. We swam in the lake, went hiking, toasted marshmallows, and ate till we were stuffed. So far, so good, right? Then I remembered why I hate nature. I came face-to-face with a skunk. And the skunk won. Before I could run away, it sprayed me. I smelled worse than anything I had ever smelled before. After the rest of the Scouts got through cracking up, they kicked me out of the tent. They said I smelled so bad, they wouldn't be able to sleep. So I had to drag my sleeping bag outside and sleep under the stars. Not that *I* could sleep, either. But I got back at them, I guess—because the next day, they had to spend three hours trapped in a car with me. And I promise you, I didn't smell any better!

— "Stinky" Sam

Love Letters

Usually my mom makes my lunch, but one week when she was sick, my grandmother came over to help out. I was psyched, because I knew my grandmother would probably give me some good junk food for dessert. My mom usually sticks with apple slices or something. And I was right. When I opened my lunch that afternoon, I discovered some delicious homemade chocolate muffins. Unfortunately, that wasn't all my grandmother

had included. She also sent along a note that read: "A little treat for my little love muffin." I tried to stuff it in my backpack as soon as I read it, but I wasn't quick enough. A kid next to me spotted the note, grabbed it, then jumped on a chair and read it out loud to the whole cafeteria. Guess what my new nickname is? That's right, "love muffin." Don't believe me? Check out this year's yearbook!

—Leslie

Baby Talk

YOU RATE IT! _____

When my aunt and uncle came over with their new baby, I was expecting to be pretty bored. I've never been a big fan of babies. But my new little cousin was incredibly cute! I spent the whole day playing with him, and when his diaper needed to be changed, my aunt let me help. I thought I was pretty cool, doing such a grown-up job . . . and then the cute little baby peed, right in my face. It was absolutely, positively the grossest thing that's ever happened to me in my entire life. And my own mother could barely stop laughing long enough to hand me a towel!

—Emma

MEGA-BLUNDER!
For Your Eyes Only

In my English class this year, we had to keep a daily journal, just writing down what we were thinking and doing, and all that stuff. I knew we would have to hand it in to the teacher at the end of the semester, so obviously I never wrote down what I was *really* thinking. I saved that for my real journal. I thought I was pretty clever, until the time came to hand in our journals. My *real* journal and my school journal are both in spiral-bound notebooks. I guess I should have realized that was a bad, bad idea, because I accidentally turned in my real journal to my teacher! It was so humiliating. The next day my teacher handed it back to me, whispering, "When I saw all those hearts around all the boys' names, I figured this might not be for me . . ."

—Diane

It's a Pirate's Life for Me

Last year for my birthday, I spent the day at an amusement park with a couple of my best friends. It was awesome. We went on the Ferris wheel, the Scrambler, and all of the roller coasters, and we also ate about a ton of cotton candy. Yum. For the last ride of the day, we decided to go on the Galleon, a giant pirate ship that rocked back and forth, back and forth, until it made a complete upside-down loop. From the moment the ride started, I knew I'd made a giant mistake. And all that cotton candy suddenly started to seem like a pretty bad idea. I felt really sick, but I managed to hold it together for the ride. Then, when it stopped, I was so relieved that I finally relaxed and then threw up all over myself, the ride, and my best friend. What a birthday present!

—Jenn

Temper, Temper

I have the worst temper in the world. Too bad for me, my big brother gets a big kick out of making me mad. One morning when we were home alone, he tricked me into going outside in my pajamas, then he locked me out of the house. I was standing on the front porch forever, pounding on the door and begging him to let me back in. I got madder and madder, until I had a total fit. I started stomping around and yelling at the top of my lungs. That's when Scott, the incredibly cute boy who lives next door, came out to see what was going on. As soon as I saw him, I stopped yelling and waved, trying my best to pretend that everything was normal. I guess I, and my pajamas, didn't fool him—he looked totally

freaked out and ran back inside his house. If you thought I was mad at my brother before, you should have seen me then!

—T. J.

HIS Humiliation
Perfect Pitch

I had an enormous, gigantic crush on this beautiful girl, Emma. After smiling at her in the halls for a few months, I finally got up the nerve to ask her out. I was incredibly nervous, but I knew I just had to take a deep breath and get it over

with. So I walked up to her and said hello, but I was so nervous, my voice cracked. I sounded like a girl! She started laughing and I was so embarrassed that I just ran away without saying another word. Now whenever I spot her in the hall, I run in the other direction.

—Damon

MEGA BLUNDER!
Sleepover Slipup

I was at my friend's sleepover party, and we were all hanging out in her bedroom. One of my friends started to tell a funny story about someone in our math class, and we all started laughing and laughing. And I'm almost too embarrassed to admit this, but I laughed so hard, I peed in my pants. I didn't know what to do. There was no way I could let my friends find out what happened. I don't know how I did it, but I convinced everyone that it was time to change into our pajamas and as everyone was getting up, no one noticed the big wet spot I'd left behind. A few minutes later, though, they did notice the smell. No one could figure out what had happened and I pretended to be as confused and grossed out as everyone else. I've still never told anyone what happened . . . and never will.

—Heather

SUMMER BUMMERS

WHAT'S THE BEST THING ABOUT SUMMER?

If you blush so much your face is permanently
the shade of a tomato, at least you can spend
these three months pretending you have a
sunburn. And when your face is blazing hotter and
redder than the summer sun, just remind
yourself—you may be upset, you may be totally
humiliated, but hey, at least you're on vacation!

Rescue 911

I've always liked to climb trees, the higher the
better. One day, I got up enough
nerve to climb the tallest tree in
my neighborhood. I'd climbed
about halfway up it before, but
I'd always chickened out and
had to come back down. This
time, I was determined—I was
going to make it to the top. And I
did. There was just one problem: Once I was up
there, I was too scared to come back down again!
The ground suddenly looked so far away. I didn't
know what to do. Eventually, I started calling out,
"Help! Help!" I think the first few people to hear
me must have thought I was just a very large,

very strange bird. But soon someone spotted me. They had to call the fire department to get me down! I still climb trees, but only the ones that aren't much taller than I am.

—Arielle

MEGA-BLUNDER!
Flash Flood Alert

I only met Katie this year, but I really liked her and was excited when she invited me over for dinner one night. It meant we were really getting to be friends. Her parents were very nice, the food was very good, and everything was going very smoothly until I had to use the bathroom. When I flushed the toilet, it started to overflow, and soon it was flooding the bathroom! I didn't know what to do. I just stood there in shock for a minute and then I knew I would have to go tell Katie and her parents. I was so embarrassed! Katie and her dad ran to the bathroom to try to fix things, her mother ran to call the plumber, and I just snuck out of the house and ran home. After flooding their bathroom, there was no way I would have been able to face them across the dining room table!

—Crystal

In Your Face

Kickball. I hate kickball. And here's why. My team had the field, and I was playing first base.

The first player up to the plate kicked the ball right toward me. It came hurtling at me, hit me in the face, broke my glasses, and then bounced off again. I actually managed to catch it on its way down! But did I get any credit for that? No way. The rest of my team just hooted, and the pitcher called out, "That's Emily, always using her head!"

—Emily

HE SAYS . . . I don't know what's wrong with your teammates. Obuiously the important thing is that you caught the ball. Sounds like MVP work to me!

American Idol

YOU RATE IT! _____

I love to sing, and I've always dreamed of being a rock star. Too bad I'm a terrible singer. So I only sing in my room where I'm sure no one can hear me. One day I was rocking out to the radio, singing and dancing around my room like I was in a music video. What I didn't know was that I *was* in a music video, thanks to my little brother and his handy video camera. But he didn't just tape me. He taped me, and then he stuck the video on his Web site. I got to be a rock star all right, just not the kind I was hoping for.

—Brynn

First Aid

I was going to a big party with my best friends, and the last thing I needed was a giant zit show-ing up on my forehead. So of course, that's exactly what I got. There was no way I was going out of the house with that thing. It looked like a third eye! But my best friend convinced me that I could just slap a Band-Aid

49

over it and tell everyone that I had cut myself. I took her advice, and for a while, it worked. I even started having some fun with it, making up a wild story about how I had gotten hit in the face with a hockey puck. I met this incredibly cute boy who actually plays hockey, and he was *very* impressed. But in the middle of our conversation, he started staring at my forehead and giggling. I had a sinking feeling that I knew why. I reached up to feel my forehead and the Band-Aid had fallen off. The giant zit—and my giant lie—was there for everyone to see. So much for meeting cute boys. I spent the rest of the night in the bathroom.

—Meredith

HE SAYS . . . Don't tell anyone, but guys get zits, too. Lots of them. So we understand. And who wants a girl who's perfect? Way too much pressure.

Wake-up Call

I used to sleepwalk a lot, and sometimes it got me into some hot water, or in this case, cold water. I was spending my first summer at overnight camp, and I guess I was a little nervous to be away from home. The first night, I dreamed that I was walking from camp back to my house, but it turns out that the walking part wasn't just a dream. I sleepwalked out of the bunkhouse, through the woods, and then right into the lake. *SPLASH!* That woke me up in a hurry! When I found myself in the middle of the freezing lake in my pajamas, I screamed, which woke up the rest of the camp. By the time I dragged myself out of the water, half the camp had shown up to watch. And laugh. And laugh. And laugh.

—Lali

Humiliation Helper

TOP 10 PIECES OF INFORMATION THAT MIGHT
GET YOU OUT OF EMBARRASSING SITUATIONS

Knowledge is power. That's as true for
embarrassing moments as it is for the SATs.
You never know what kind of info might
get you out of trouble, so you'd better soak
in all you can while you've got the chance.

1. **TO GET GUM OUT OF YOUR HAIR**, try
   rubbing ice on it until the gum hardens. Then
   you should be able to pick it out.

2. **SOAK STAINS IN COLD WATER,** *not*
   hot water. (Hot water may make them
   permanent!)

3. **BEFORE YOU STICK ANY HAIR DYE IN
   YOUR HAIR**, test a little of the dye on your
   hand first, just in case you have a bad reaction.

4. **IF YOU'VE BEEN SPRAYED BY A SKUNK**, taking a bath in tomato juice will *not* help you get rid of the stink. It will just leave you smelly *and* orange.

5. **DON'T SHAKE UP YOUR CAN OF SODA**. When you open it, it will explode.

6. **GOOD DINNERS CAN SOMETIMES MEAN BAD BREATH**. Out of breath mints? Try chewing some parsley. It won't taste great, but it'll clean up your mouth ASAP.

7. **WHEN IT COMES TO MAKEUP**, less is *always* better than more.

8. **YOU SHOULD NEVER POP YOUR ZITS** — it can leave scars. Zits will eventually disappear . . . scars never will.

9. **IF YOU HATE YOUR HAIRCUT**, go back to the salon and complain—many places will give you a new cut for free.

10. **THERE'S NO SUCH THING** as privacy on the Internet. So if you don't want the world to read it, think twice before you send it.

HIS Humiliation
Look Who's Talking

YOU RATE IT! _____

When my older brother Mike started dating the most beautiful girl in school, was I jealous? You bet. But I believe in looking on the bright side, and here it was: If my brother dated her, that meant I would probably get to meet her. Maybe even talk to her! And then one day, it happened: I answered the phone, and it was *her*. When I told her that Mike wasn't home, she left a message and then said those magic words: "So, what's your name?" Before I could answer, she kept going: "I didn't even know Mike *had* a little sister." Uh, he doesn't—just a little brother with a very high voice. Now whenever she comes over, I have to hide in my room!

—David

Bugging Out

It was my first day at camp, and everything was going great. I loved the counselors, I loved the campers, and I really loved beating the guys' camp at volleyball that morning. Then we had our first afternoon snack—cookies and "bug juice." I totally freaked out! The other kids in my bunk all started drinking it like they didn't care. That's when my counselor had to explain it to me: "Bug juice" doesn't have *real* bugs in it. It's just what they called the fruit punch. I knew then that it was going to be a lo-o-o-o-o-ong summer.

—**Tina**

Better Late than Never

On the last day of school, our teacher handed out our report cards, and I couldn't wait to take a look at mine. I ripped open the envelope and— yes! Straight A's. I was psyched, but then I noticed that I had a bunch of "tardy" marks at the bottom. I didn't know what that meant, but it didn't sound good. I raised my hand and asked the teacher why I was marked "tardy." She checked her records and told me that I had been late six times. That was true, I said, but so what? I had never been tardy. The whole class started laughing and that's when she explained "late" and "tardy" meant the same thing. Despite all those A's, I felt pretty dumb.

—Natalya

To Bee, or Not to Bee

YOU RATE IT! _____

We were doing a ropes course at Girl Scout camp, and since I'm afraid of heights, I wasn't too happy about it. But when it was my turn, I psyched myself up and climbed up onto the rope bridge. I was terrified and then things got worse. Much, much worse. In the middle of my very shaky walk across the bridge, I saw a bee. I'm about a million times more afraid of bees than I am of heights and this bee was coming right at me. I started flailing around, trying to get it away from me, which only made it want to sting me more. Which it did. I screamed and backed away, knocking myself off balance, and right off the rope bridge. Everyone was watching and laughing. I sprained my ankle *and* my ego.

—Rina

Feeling Hot, Hot, Hot

During the heat wave this summer, I rode my bike to my friend's house to go swimming. It was so hot that I thought maybe I should leave my bike in the garage instead of out on the driveway. But she told me it was fine, so I left it there and we went to take a swim. When I came back to the front of the house at the end of the afternoon, I found my bike lying in the driveway with the front tire completely twisted out of shape. We couldn't figure out what had happened but finally decided that it must have melted in the sun! The next day at camp, I told everyone how my bike had melted. They didn't believe me, but I swore it was true. Then I got home and found out that my friend's mother had called to apologize. The day before, she had pulled her car into the driveway and accidentally ran over my bike. No wonder no one believed me!

—Lindsay

MEGA-BLUNDER!
Not So Happy Hour

On our school trip last year, we got to stay overnight at a hotel. It was great—the first time I've ever been at a hotel without my parents. The best part was happy hour, when we got all the free appetizers and soft drinks we could eat. And I can eat a lot. Seven glasses of soda and about a million mini-hot dogs later, I wasn't feeling so great. Our teacher came over to see why I was looking so green, and I threw up all over her. It was *so* embarrassing and *so* lame that I had to stay in bed the rest of the night.

—Prashi

HIS Humiliation
Lady Liberty

The best vacation I ever had was the week my family spent in New York City. It's the greatest city on earth, and every minute of our trip was perfect. Well, *almost* every minute. There was the day we spent at the Statue of Liberty. We waited in line for *five hours* before we could start our way up the incredibly narrow staircase. We walked and walked and walked and walked and walked. And then, about a third of the way up, my mother decided she was more afraid of heights than she'd thought. So afraid, in fact, that she needed to get down. Right away. The stairs are so narrow that there's no room for people to go in two different directions, so before we could get down, the hundred people behind us had to get down. Backwards. By the time we made it to the ground, there was a giant crowd of people waiting for us to get by and looking like they wanted to throw us into the river.

—Derek

Ay Carumba!

Last year for my birthday, my parents took me to my favorite Mexican restaurant. I love spicy food, and that place has the spiciest food in town. Dinner was great—warm chips, delicious salsa, and a giant plate of enchiladas with hot pepper sauce. Everything was perfect until I accidentally swallowed a whole pepper. My mouth was on fire and all our water was gone! I didn't know what to do. My face was turning red and I felt like the top of my head was going to explode, like in the cartoons. I couldn't stand it anymore. I jumped up from the table and grabbed a glass of water off the table next to us. But I was in such a hurry to drink it that I spilled it all over myself! Finally, I got some into my mouth. Ahhhh. I was so relieved that it took me a minute to realize that the entire restaurant was staring at me. And not because it was my birthday!

—Helen

How I Learned to Stop Worrying and Live My Life . . .

You may wonder how I make it through each day, knowing that the possibility of **absolute humiliation** lurks around every corner. . . .

Well, I just do it. That's how.

I realized a long time ago that there's nothing I can do to keep myself free of embarrassing moments. No matter how careful you are to stay clear of **banana peels**, **puddles**, and pesky **little brothers**, there's always something out there waiting to trip you up or knock you down. And, if you have the kind of luck I do (by which I mean **BAD** luck), there's probably someone standing, watching, and laughing as you fall flat on your face.

My strategy? **Laugh right along** with them. Even if I don't find the whole thing funny at all, I just pick myself up, laugh as hard as I can under the circumstances, and then move on with my life.

You may not believe me, but sometimes it actually **works**. Suddenly I'm laughing for real, and being embarrassed doesn't seem so terrible after all.

And then there are those times that it doesn't work. The times that I wouldn't come out of my room and show my face to the world for a million dollars. The times that I've embarrassed myself in front of everyone I know and begged my parents to let me switch schools. The times that I think I'll be feeling this way **forever**.

But each of those times, I've been wrong. **Embarrassment stinks**. But it also disappears. It may take an hour, it may take a week, but eventually, it'll be gone, and you can move on with the rest of your life.

So I say, **why fear humiliation**? Embarrassment is here today and gone tomorrow. It's everything else, all the good stuff in life, like friends, family, and chocolate cookies, that's here to stay.

And take it from me,

it's the good stuff that counts!